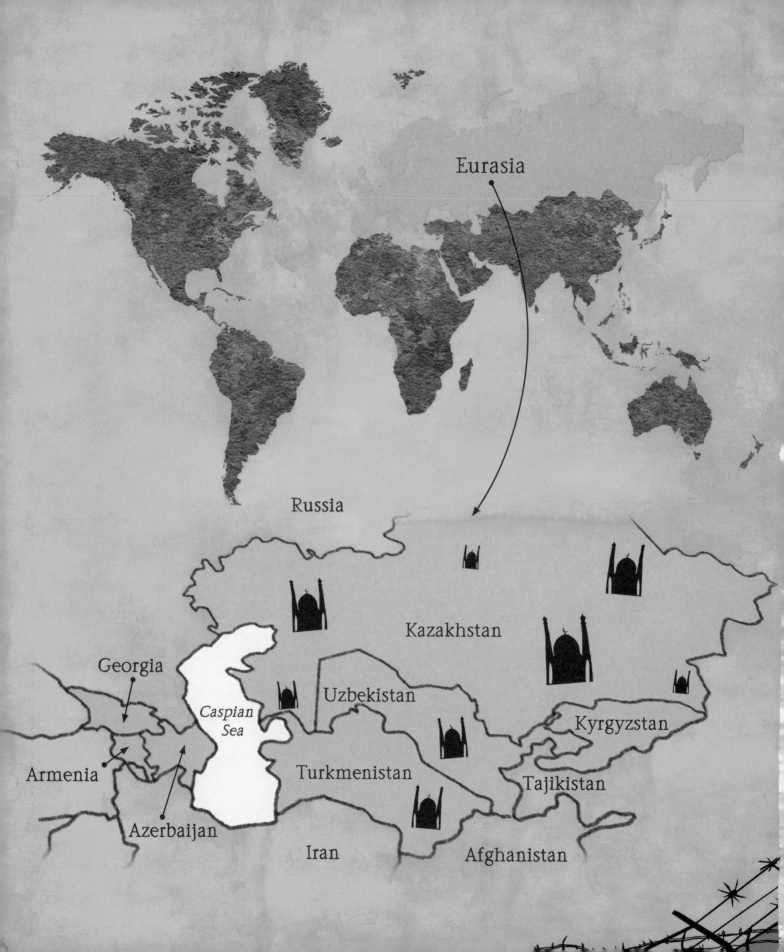

# RACHEL'S STORY...

A **real-life** account of her journey
from a country in Eurasia

Created by
Andy Glynne and
Salvador Maldonado

First published in 2014 by Wayland

Text and Illustrations © Mosaic Films 2014

Wayland, 338 Euston Road, London NW1 3BH

Wayland Australia, Level 17/207, Kent Street, Sydney, NSW 2000

Mosaic Films, Shacklewell Lane, London E8 2EZ

Conceived by Andy Glynne
Designed by Salvador Maldonado
Artwork by Tine Mette Jespersen,
Tom Clohosy Cole and Alexandre Belbari
Additional artwork by Simon Swales

Editor: Debbie Foy
Designer: Sophie Wilkins

Dewey ref:  362.7'7914'092-dc23

ISBN 978 0 7502 7888 1
eBook ISBN 978 0 7502 9374 7

Lib eBook ISBN 978 0 7502 7893 5

Printed in China

10 9 8 7 6 5 4 3 2 1

Wayland is a division of Hachette Children's Books,
an Hachette UK company.

www.hachette.co.uk

# RACHEL'S STORY...

## My name is Rachel.

This is the story of my journey
from a country in Eurasia.

WAYLAND
www.waylandbooks.co.uk

Life in my country was quite distressing.

I didn't go to school because my mum
practised a different religion from
most of the other people.

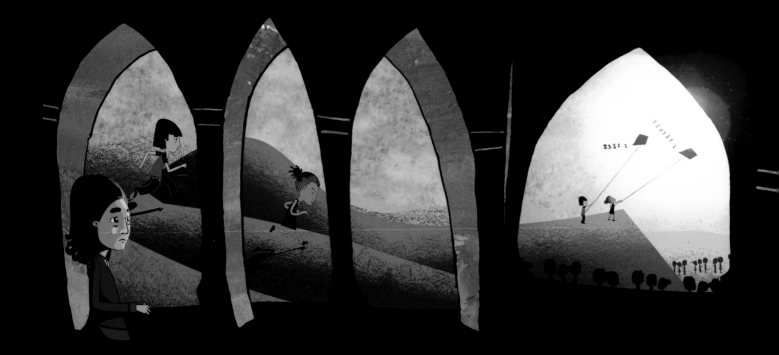

I could see other children around
me having a normal childhood.
They would go to school or play
outside with their friends,
but I felt very different.

In many countries, being a Christian isn't a problem but in my country it wasn't an accepted religion or tradition.

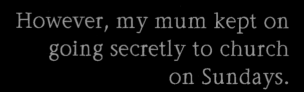

However, my mum kept on going secretly to church on Sundays.

When the police invaded
the secret church services,
the situation became very
difficult and dangerous.

Our lives changed over night and
my mum was treated very badly by the
local people. She felt like she really
wanted to escape.

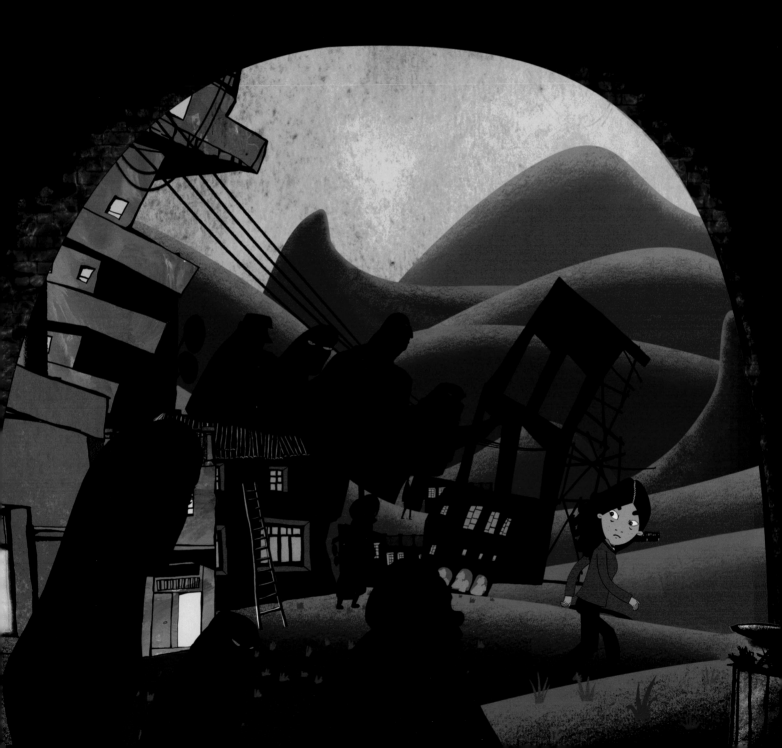

We secretly decided to leave.
We didn't let anyone know. My dad
found someone who would take
us in the back of his lorry.

All three of us clutched each other tightly as we travelled.
We slept and slept. It was very dark so we couldn't see
whether it was day or night.

We totally lost track of time.
We had no idea where we were
going or where we'd end up.

Eventually we arrived in our new country.
Gradually I started to have the kind of
childhood that I'd always dreamt of.

I had friends. I played outside safely
and we had a normal family life.

But then the letter came that changed everything.
It said that our appeal for leave to remain in our new
country had been rejected. This single piece of
paper changed my whole life all over again!

At 6 o'clock the next morning, some great big men,
like huge monsters, came to our house.
They put us in a van and took
us to a detention centre.

We could hear doors banging all the time in the detention centre. It had huge walls. We couldn't see outside – everything was closed up.

I remember looking up
at the high wall and wishing
that I could just fly over
it and escape!

I remember holding the bars in my hands.
I couldn't believe that I was stuck in
a prison, in a foreign country,
for doing nothing wrong.

A little while later,
we were allowed out of
the detention centre.

But I was always afraid that the
same thing would happen again.

And it did...

This time the
authorities took us straight
to the airport. We were
put on a plane back
to our country.

Our people didn't welcome us at all. They looked at us with hostility and hatred. They blamed us for leaving and going to a foreign country.

One day my mum fainted because someone hit her across the head.

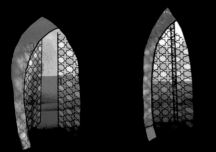

My family and I travelled
everywhere searching for help,
but with no success. So my
mum decided we had to
leave once again.

She found us an agent who helped us
and soon we were able to escape.

Back in our new
country the people were
very kind and welcoming.
Finally I felt safe.

We lived a normal life but
deep down I always had
the fear inside me that
something dreadful
could happen at
any time.

Then one day we got a phone call. I thought it was bad news, but the lady on the other end said that she had good news. We had been granted leave to remain in our new country. We were overjoyed!

That was the phone
call that changed
my whole life
forever!

LAWYER'S OFFICE

I've learnt from my experience. I've decided that I want to study law so that I can help people who have the same kinds of problems

Sadly, people are still suffering
everywhere in the world, but when
I become an international lawyer,
hopefully I can save
everyone!

The complete **SEEKING REFUGE** series.

Real-life testimonies of young refugees fleeing their homelands.

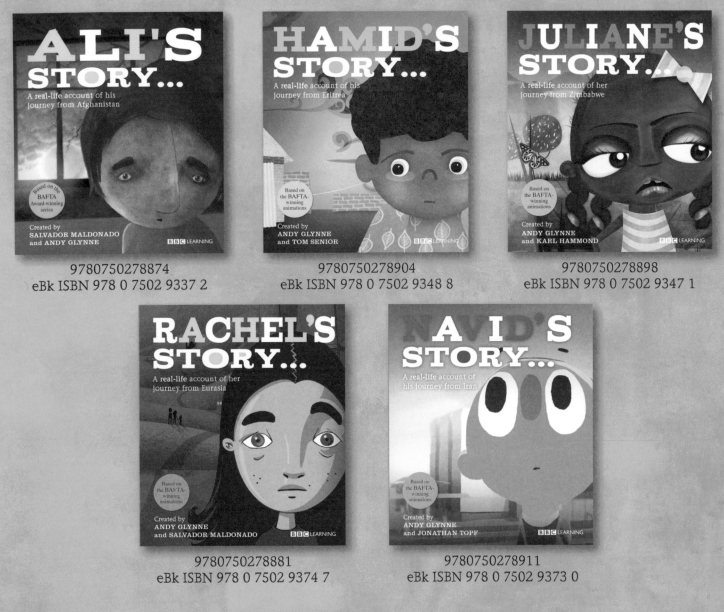

9780750278874
eBk ISBN 978 0 7502 9337 2

9780750278904
eBk ISBN 978 0 7502 9348 8

9780750278898
eBk ISBN 978 0 7502 9347 1

9780750278881
eBk ISBN 978 0 7502 9374 7

9780750278911
eBk ISBN 978 0 7502 9373 0

Available only from WAYLAND

WAYLAND
www.waylandbooks.co.uk